COUNTRY EXPLORERS

COSTA RICA

Tracey West

Lerner Publications Company • Minneapolis

Lerner Publications Company
A division of Lerner Publishing Group, Inc.
241 First Avenue North
Minneapolis, MN 55401 U.S.A.

Website address: www.lernerbooks.com

Library of Congress Cataloging-in-Publication Data

West, Tracey, 1965–
 Costa Rica / by Tracey West.
   p.   cm. — (Country explorers)
 Includes index.
 ISBN 978–0–8225–9416–1 (lib. bdg. : alk. paper)
 1. Costa Rica—Juvenile literature. I. Title.
 F1543.2.W47 2009
 972.86—dc22   2007042166

Manufactured in the United States of America
1 2 3 4 5 6 – PA – 14 13 12 11 10 09

Table of Contents

Costa Rica

Welcome!

Costa Rica is a small country in Central America. This is a string of countries that links the continents of North America and South America.

Costa Rica lies between two other Central American countries. Nicaragua is to the north. Panama sits to the southeast. Costa Rica acts like a bridge between them. Water is everywhere else. The Caribbean Sea splashes the northeastern coast of Costa Rica. The Pacific Ocean crashes onto its western and southwestern shores.

Waves wash the shore of a beach in Corcovado National Park. The park is on the Osa Peninsula in southern Costa Rica.

4

NICARAGUA

SAN JUAN RIVER

MILES
0   50

KILOMETERS
0   50

TORTUGUERO
NATIONAL PARK

CARIBBEAN
SEA

Liberia

Lake
Arenal

ARENAL VOLCANO
NATIONAL PARK

C O S T A

PLAYA
GRANDE

NICOYA
PENINSULA

BRAULIO CARRILLO
NATIONAL PARK

CENTRAL

San José ★

Guayabo

PLATEAU

Puerto Limón

Ostional

R I C A

Cahuita
CAHUITA
NATIONAL PARK

Puerto Viejo

PLAYA
HERMOSA

PACIFIC
OCEAN

PANAMA

rain forest
mountains
highlands
protected areas
volcanoes
country's capital

OSA
PENINSULA

N

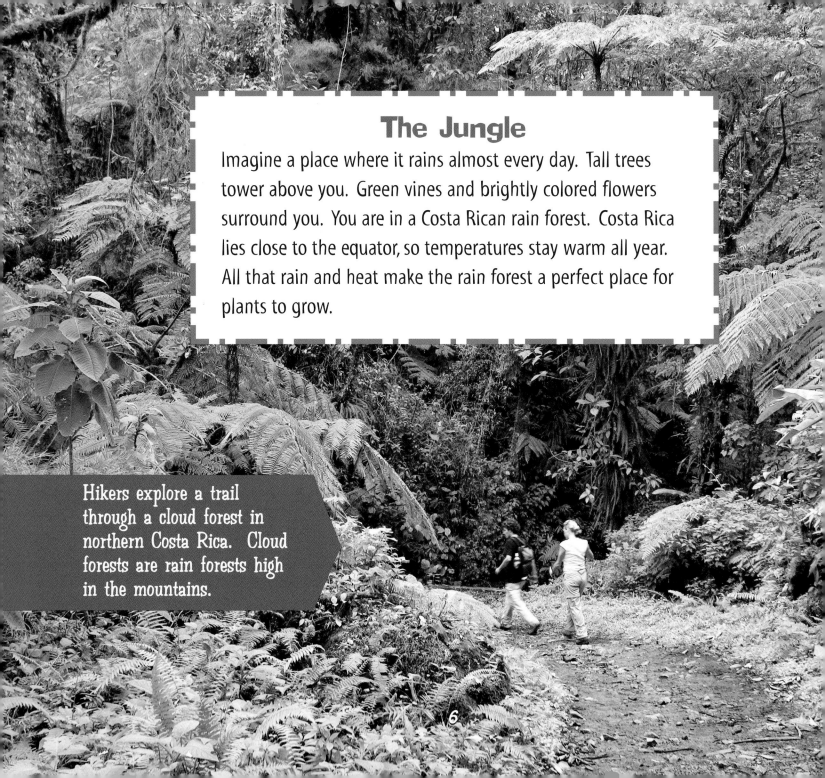

The Jungle

Imagine a place where it rains almost every day. Tall trees tower above you. Green vines and brightly colored flowers surround you. You are in a Costa Rican rain forest. Costa Rica lies close to the equator, so temperatures stay warm all year. All that rain and heat make the rain forest a perfect place for plants to grow.

Hikers explore a trail through a cloud forest in northern Costa Rica. Cloud forests are rain forests high in the mountains.

Many animals also live in Costa Rica's rain forests. Ants carry leaves along the ground. Sloths and monkeys hang from branches. Birds such as toucans, parrots, and quetzals fly through the treetops.

Map Whiz Quiz

Trace the outline of Costa Rica onto a sheet of paper. Find Nicaragua. Label that area of your paper with an *N* for north. Put an *S* for south in the Pacific Ocean near Panama. Do you see the Nicoya Peninsula? Mark that with a *W* for west. The Caribbean Sea gets an *E* for east on your map. Use a green crayon to shade in Costa Rica's protected areas.

Colorful parrots, such as these scarlet macaws, live in Costa Rica's rain forests.

Hot liquid rock called lava flows from Arenal Volcano. It lies in the mountains north of the Central Valley.

Up High

Rain forests line Costa Rica's low, flat coasts. Further inland, mountains push up the land. They ring the Central Valley. In the middle of the valley lies the Central Plateau.

More than one hundred of Costa Rica's mountains are volcanoes. But few still erupt or blow up. Lava and ash from the volcanoes become part of the soil. Over hundreds of years, layers and layers of lava and ash have turned the Central Valley into rich farmland.

This farmland is near the capital city of San José.

Christopher Columbus sailed four times to North America and South America. On his fourth voyage, he landed in Costa Rica.

Land, Ho!

Long ago, the explorer Christopher Columbus and his crew first set eyes on Costa Rica. They met *indigenas* (native peoples) who lived there. The explorers admired their beautiful clothing and gold jewelry. The explorers hoped to find great wealth in the new land. So they called the area Costa Rica. That means "rich coast" in the Spanish language.

Later, other people from Spain came in search of gold. They did not find much. But some stayed to farm Costa Rica's rich soil. Most Costa Ricans can trace their long-ago family to Spanish settlers or to indigenas. People of mixed Spanish and indigena backgrounds are called mestizos.

Children from a village near Puntarenas

11

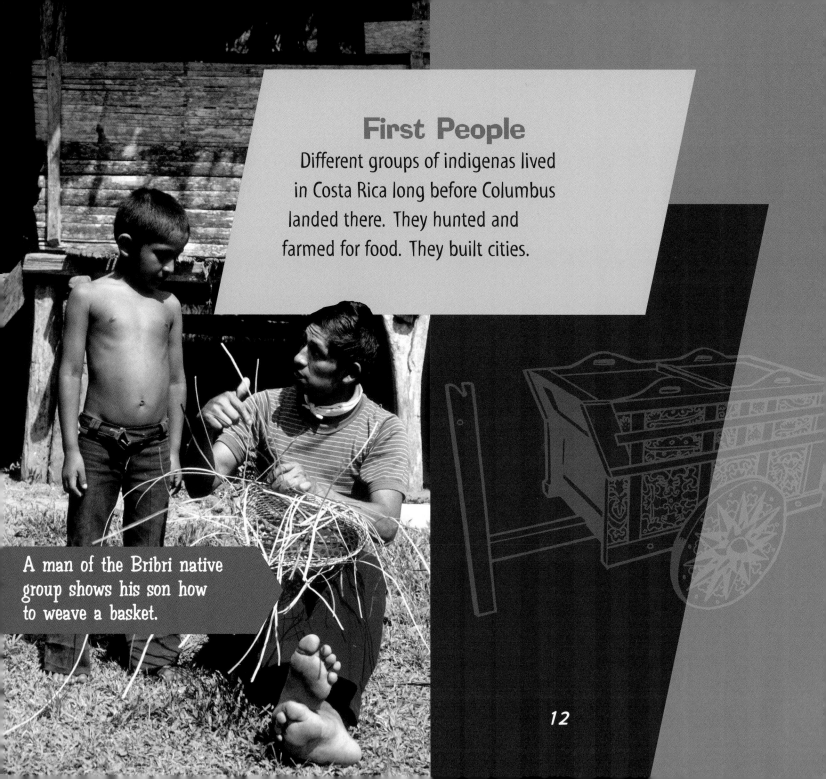

First People

Different groups of indigenas lived in Costa Rica long before Columbus landed there. They hunted and farmed for food. They built cities.

A man of the Bribri native group shows his son how to weave a basket.

12

These indigena children live in a village in the mountains of southern Costa Rica.

Mystery Town

Long, long ago, an indigena group lived near the present-day town of Guayabo. Six hundred years ago, the people left. But parts of their village still remain. Winding stone roads and rising pillars remind visitors of the town's past. Scientists study the town to learn about how these early Costa Ricans lived. Still, no one knows for sure who built this town or why they left it.

These days, only about ten thousand indigenas still live in Costa Rica. Most live in small communities or on land set aside by the government.

Jungle Train

In the late 1800s, a railroad was built to link the cities of San José and Puerto Limón. Thousands of people came from other countries to help lay tracks through the jungle. Workers from Britain, Jamaica, Italy, and China added to the mix of Costa Ricans.

The families of these children came from Jamaica. They settled in the southeastern town of Puerto Viejo.

Recent newcomers to Costa Rica include people from Nicaragua. Many come to find jobs on Costa Rica's coffee and banana farms.

Ticos

Costa Ricans have nicknamed themselves *ticos*. A popular saying in Costa Rica is *todos somos ticos*—"we are all Costa Ricans." This means that everyone in the country is proud to be Costa Rican. It doesn't matter where a person's original family came from.

A Costa Rican man shows Nicaraguan workers which rows of coffee beans to pick.

15

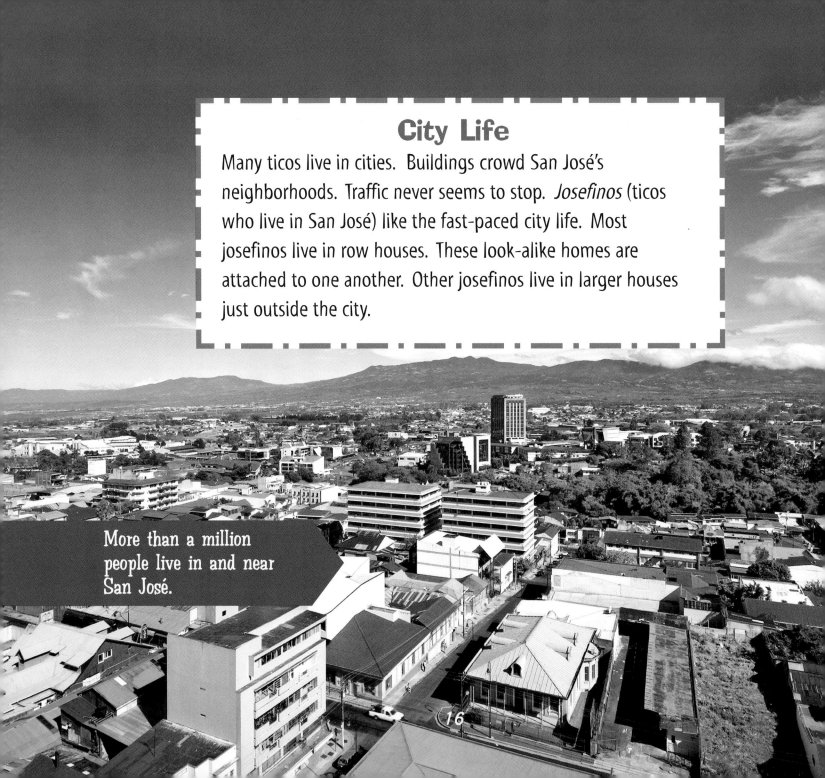

City Life

Many ticos live in cities. Buildings crowd San José's neighborhoods. Traffic never seems to stop. *Josefinos* (ticos who live in San José) like the fast-paced city life. Most josefinos live in row houses. These look-alike homes are attached to one another. Other josefinos live in larger houses just outside the city.

More than a million people live in and near San José.

16

Dear Grandpa,

San José is fun! Yesterday we spent the morning in La Plaza de la Cultura. People sell all kinds of crafts there. Mom let me pick out a bamboo flute. We watched magicians, storytellers, and musicians perform. After lunch, we stopped at the Gold Museum. Everything we saw was made thousands of years ago! Tomorrow we are going on a hike through a rain forest. See you soon!

Love,
Abigail

Gr
An
Anyu

San José

Campesinos

Campesinos are people who live in the countryside. Some campesinos live in large, colorful houses. Others build small cottages out of a kind of brick called adobe.

Campesinos meet or gather in the plaza. It's usually in the center of town. Another place to hang out is *la pulpería*. At these stores, people can buy everything from hardware to candy.

This country home lies near Arenal Volcano.

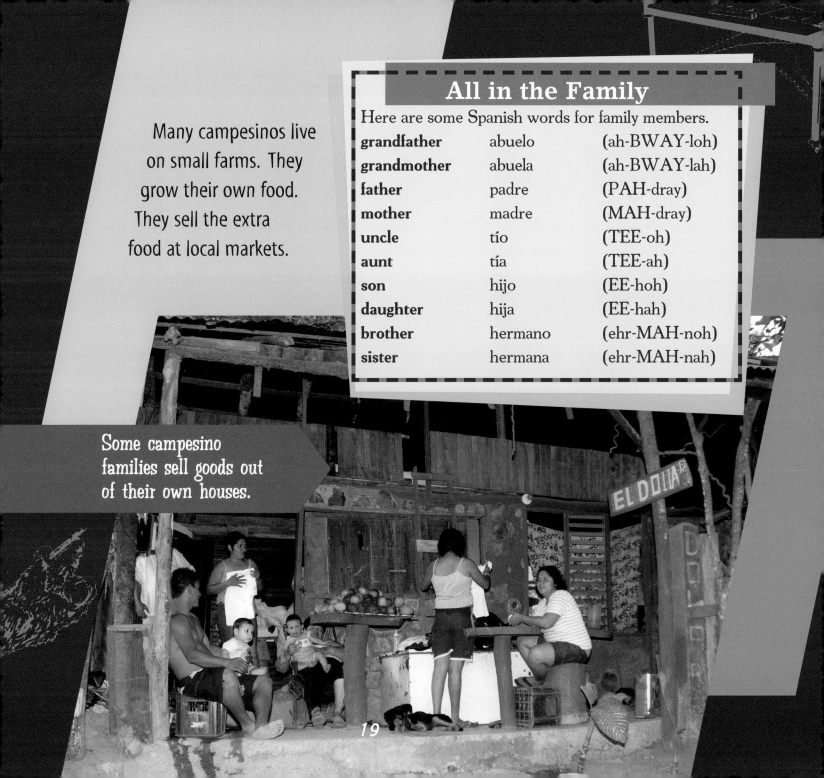

Many campesinos live on small farms. They grow their own food. They sell the extra food at local markets.

All in the Family

Here are some Spanish words for family members.

English	Spanish	Pronunciation
grandfather	abuelo	(ah-BWAY-loh)
grandmother	abuela	(ah-BWAY-lah)
father	padre	(PAH-dray)
mother	madre	(MAH-dray)
uncle	tío	(TEE-oh)
aunt	tía	(TEE-ah)
son	hijo	(EE-hoh)
daughter	hija	(EE-hah)
brother	hermano	(ehr-MAH-noh)
sister	hermana	(ehr-MAH-nah)

Some campesino families sell goods out of their own houses.

19

School Days

Get out your books! Costa Rican kids between the ages of six and fifteen go to school. Getting dressed in the morning is a snap. Everybody wears a uniform to school.

Students pose for a photo in their school uniforms.

Students study reading, math, and social studies. Classes learn about taking care of the environment too. Kids are taught to protect the rain forest in their own neighborhoods!

Schoolchildren in Costa Rica learn about the rain forest.

Food

What's for breakfast? How about a plate of *gallo pinto?* (That's black beans and rice.) *Gallo pinto* means "spotted rooster." The dish gets its name because it's black and white—just like a rooster!

Gallo pinto can be served with any Costa Rican meal, including breakfast. It is the national dish of Costa Rica.

At lunch or dinner, ticos may eat tortillas stuffed with beef, chicken, beans, or pork. A special treat is *la olla*. It's a soup made of beef and vegetables.

Tropical Fruit

Bananas, mangoes, papayas, and pineapples make tasty desserts. Many ticos can pick tropical fruits from trees in their own backyards!

A roadside stand sells many kinds of locally grown fruit.

23

Religion

Most Costa Ricans are Roman Catholic. Spanish settlers brought this religion with them when they came to Costa Rica. Jamaicans brought the Protestant religion to Costa Rica. Some indígenas practice their traditional religions.

Every year, thousands of people visit this Catholic church in Cartago near San José.

24

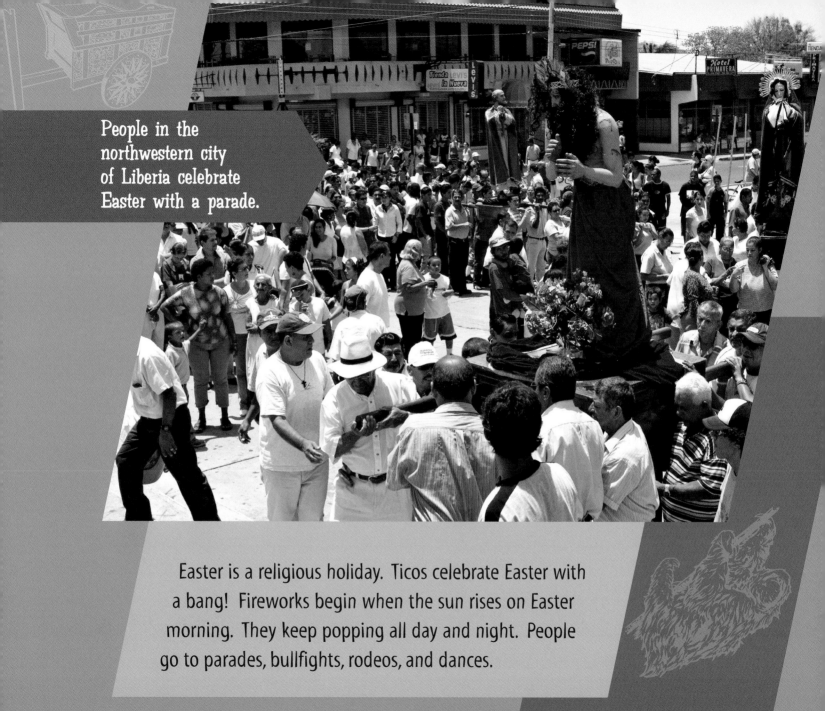

People in the
northwestern city
of Liberia celebrate
Easter with a parade.

Easter is a religious holiday. Ticos celebrate Easter with
a bang! Fireworks begin when the sun rises on Easter
morning. They keep popping all day and night. People
go to parades, bullfights, rodeos, and dances.

Ticos in Puerto Limón hold big celebrations on Día de la Raza (Columbus Day).

Proud to Be Tico

Ticos are proud of their country and its history. They celebrate special days with parades and parties. Columbus Day is the biggest holiday. Celebrations last for four days. Ticos remember the long-ago day when Christopher Columbus arrived in their land.

Costa Ricans take election days seriously. Everyone comes out to vote and to celebrate. People dip their thumbs in purple ink to show that they voted.

Ticos celebrate their independence from Spain on September 15. The sashes on these girls' costumes name different Costa Rican towns.

27

What Army?

Costa Rica is a peaceful country. It doesn't have an army. Instead, it has a national guard. The guard patrols the streets during national events.

The coast guard helps catch lawbreakers in the waters near Costa Rica.

A Costa Rican Boy Scout carries food that will help feed flood victims.

29

Listen to the Music!

Tico music blends the sounds of the indigenas, the Caribbean peoples, and the Spaniards. Sway to the tunes of indigena instruments! The *chirimia* is like an oboe (an instrument that makes a high-pitched sound). The *quijongo* has one string and a hollow bowl that makes sounds when the string is plucked.

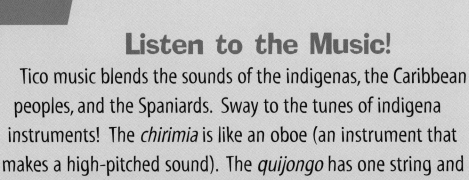

These ticos are performing a traditional dance.

The marimba has a fun and funky sound. This huge xylophone has wooden bars arranged like piano keys. Musicians strike the bars with mallets. Guitar players often strum along with marimba music.

Three musicians play together on this marimba. Two other musicians add to the mix.

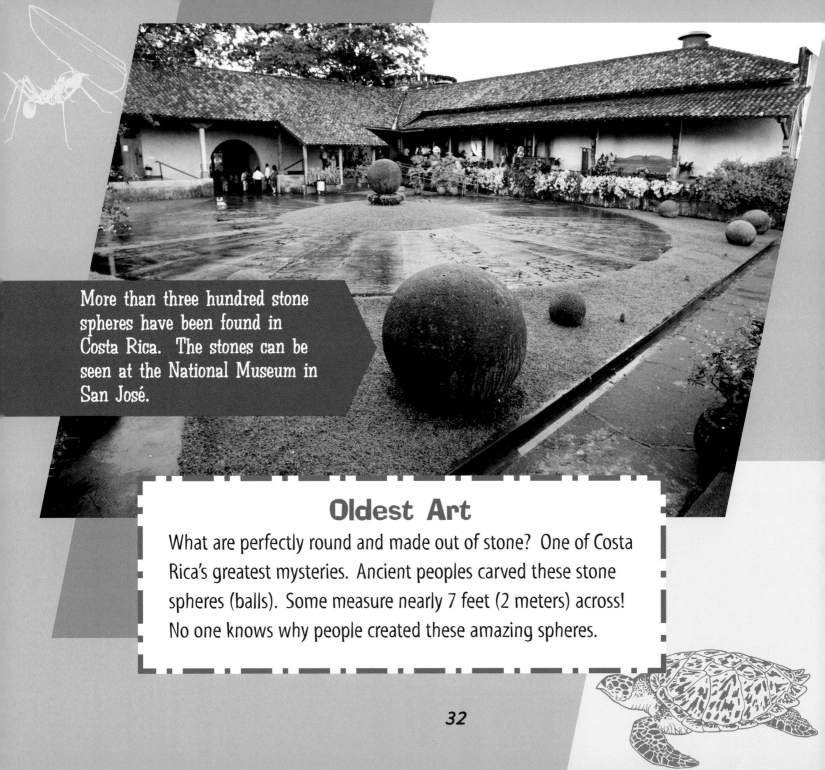

More than three hundred stone spheres have been found in Costa Rica. The stones can be seen at the National Museum in San José.

Oldest Art

What are perfectly round and made out of stone? One of Costa Rica's greatest mysteries. Ancient peoples carved these stone spheres (balls). Some measure nearly 7 feet (2 meters) across! No one knows why people created these amazing spheres.

The painted *carreta* (oxcart) is one of Costa Rica's famous art forms. Ticos once used oxcarts to transport coffee beans over mountain roads. Trucks and trains have replaced the oxcart. But artists still paint the colorful wagons.

Carretas are painted with beautiful patterns and shapes.

Playtime!

Costa Rica has plenty of fun things to do. Ticos might make special trips to San José to see a play. Northwestern Costa Rica is famous for its rodeo contests. Cowboys ride on the backs of bulls, while the animals buck and kick. Hang on tight!

Kids go to the movies or watch TV. Some kids go to the beach. Others are taking up baseball. But all ticos are crazy about fútbol.

A man enters a bull ring during a rodeo.

Neighborhood boys gather for a friendly game of *fútbol* (soccer).

Fútbol means "soccer" in Spanish. Kids play fútbol whenever and wherever they can. Any open spot can become a fútbol field. Professionals play at the national stadium in San José.

La Playa

In Costa Rica, *la playa* (the beach) is never far away. Ticos who want to check out sea turtles can go to Playa Grande. Surfers prefer Playa Hermosa.

Beaches near the Pacific Ocean are popular places for surfers in Costa Rica.

Scuba divers head to the beach near Cahuita. They swim in the clear waters of the Caribbean Sea. They can see beautiful fish and other sea life.

This beach is part of Cahuita National Park.

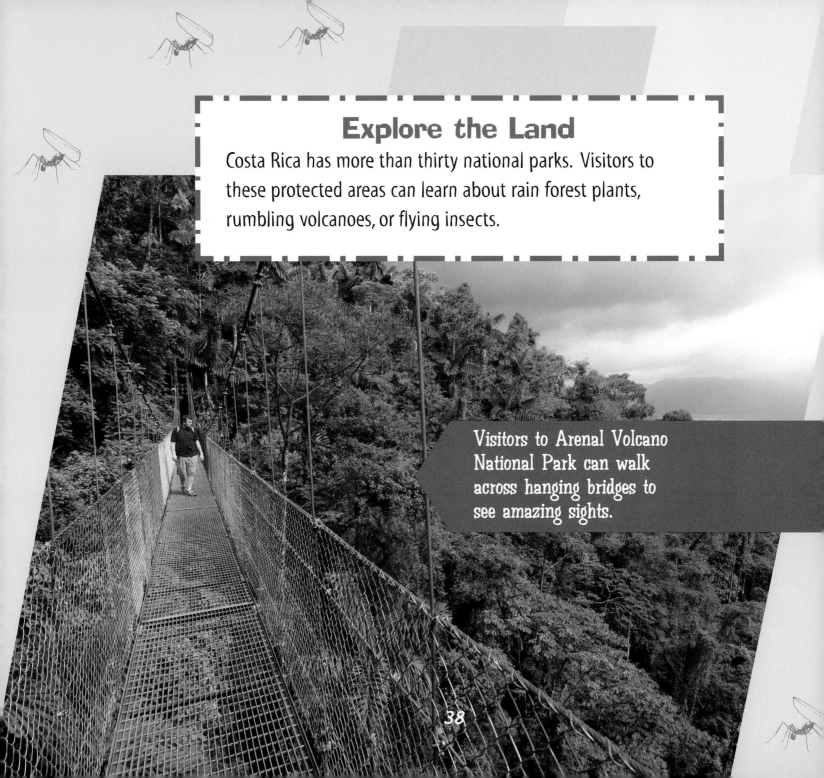

Explore the Land

Costa Rica has more than thirty national parks. Visitors to these protected areas can learn about rain forest plants, rumbling volcanoes, or flying insects.

Visitors to Arenal Volcano National Park can walk across hanging bridges to see amazing sights.

People visiting Braulio Carrillo National Park can ride high above the rain forest in a cable car. Jungles, waterfalls, and coconut trees cover Cocos Island National Park.

Sharks!

Visitors come to Cocos Island to see its great beauty. Scuba divers get a close look at underwater caves. Hammerhead and white-tipped sharks swim near the coast. Divers may see hundreds of sharks at once!

This scuba diver swims after a white-tipped reef shark in the waters off Cocos Island.

Turtle Tales

Every year, female sea turtles crawl up the beach near the village of Ostional. They lay their eggs in the warm sand. In two months, thousands of baby turtles hatch from the eggs and flop to the sea.

Baby olive ridley sea turtles cross the sandy beach to the Pacific Ocean.

Not all the eggs survive. Animals dig up many of them. The villagers of Ostional protect the nests. When the eggs hatch, the villagers make sure the baby turtles get to sea safely.

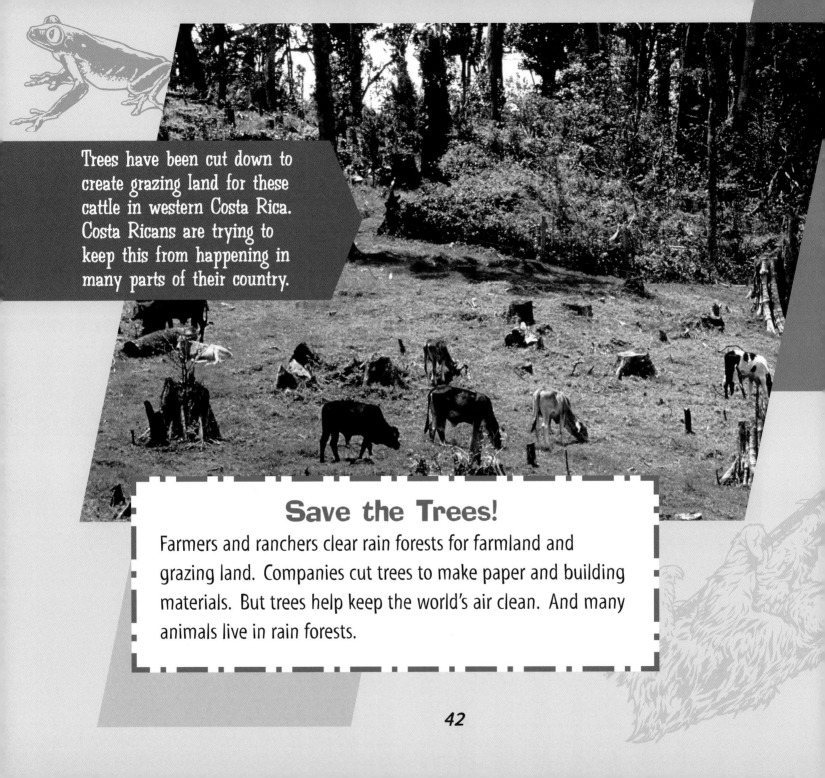

Trees have been cut down to create grazing land for these cattle in western Costa Rica. Costa Ricans are trying to keep this from happening in many parts of their country.

Save the Trees!

Farmers and ranchers clear rain forests for farmland and grazing land. Companies cut trees to make paper and building materials. But trees help keep the world's air clean. And many animals live in rain forests.

Some Costa Ricans want to protect the rain forests. The Costa Rican government turns some rain forest land into parks and protected areas. No one can cut down trees in these places.

Ecotourists can stay at this lodge at Tortuguero National Park.

THE FLAG OF COSTA RICA

Costa Rica's flag is blue, white, and red. The blue stripes stand for the sky and the country's spirit. The white stripes represent peace. The red stripe stands for the blood shed for Costa Rica's independence. On the left side of the red stripe is a small, white circle. In that circle is Costa Rica's coat of arms. A coat of arms is a design that has symbols that are important to a country or a family. Costa Rica's coat of arms has ships sailing on two oceans and three volcanoes on a green island.

FAST FACTS

FULL COUNTRY NAME: República de Costa Rica (Republic of Costa Rica)

AREA: 19,929 square miles (51,616 square kilometers), or about the size of Vermont and New Hampshire combined

MAIN LANDFORMS: the mountain ranges Guanacaste, Tilarán, Talamanca, and Central; the volcanoes Barva, Arenal, Irazú, Poás, and Tenorio; the peninsulas Nicoya and Osa; the Caribbean Lowlands; the Central Valley

MAJOR RIVERS: San Juan

ANIMALS AND THEIR HABITATS: bats, monkeys, raccoons, pumas, sloths, deer, iguanas, frogs, boa constrictors, leaf-cutter ants, butterflies, harpy eagles, toucans, parakeets (rain forest), anteaters (forest and grassland), crocodiles (swamps and rivers), sea turtles, dolphins, sharks (ocean)

CAPITAL CITY: San José

OFFICIAL LANGUAGE: Spanish

POPULATION: about 4,500,000

GLOSSARY

Central America: the narrow southern part of North America that connects it to South America. The countries of Central America are Guatemala, El Salvador, Honduras, Nicaragua, Costa Rica, Panama, and Belize.

continent: any one of seven large areas of land. The continents are Africa, Antarctica, Asia, Australia, Europe, North America, and South America.

equator: the imaginary line that circles a globe's middle and is halfway between the North Pole and the South Pole

lava: hot, liquid rock that comes out of an erupting volcano

map: a drawing or chart of all or part of Earth or the sky

peninsula: a piece of land that has water on three of its sides. The fourth side is connected to land.

plateau: a large area of high, level land

plaza: a public square, usually located near the center of a town

rain forest: a thick, green forest that gets lots of rain every year

rodeo: a contest usually performed on horseback. Rodeo events include roping calves and riding bulls.

volcano: an opening in Earth's surface through which hot, melted rock shoots up. The word volcano can also mean the hill or mountain of ash and rock that builds up around the opening.

TO LEARN MORE

BOOKS

Deady, Kathleen W. *Costa Rica*. New York: Children's Press, 2004. This book takes a look at life in Costa Rica.

Gale Group. *Into Wild Costa Rica*. San Diego: Blackbirch Press, 2004. Follow Animal Planet host Jeff Corwin as he travels across Costa Rica, meeting a host of wild animals on his journey.

Keister, Douglas. *Fernando's Gift*. San Francisco: Sierra Club Books for Children, 1995. A young boy and his family struggle to save their home in the rain forest.

Pratt-Serafini, Kristin Joy, and Rachel Crandell. *The Forever Forest: Kids Save a Tropical Treasure*. Nevada City, CA: Dawn Publications, 2008. Read about the plants and animals that live in the Children's Eternal Rain Forest in Costa Rica.

WEBSITES

Costa Rican Children's Songs—Costa Rica—Mama Lisa's World
http://www.mamalisa.com/world/costaric.html
Learn the Spanish and English words to several kids' songs from Costa Rica.

Kids Saving the Rain Forest
http://www.kidssavingtherainforest.org
This website shows what kids can do to help protect and save the rain forest.

INDEX